The Invasion
of the Crow

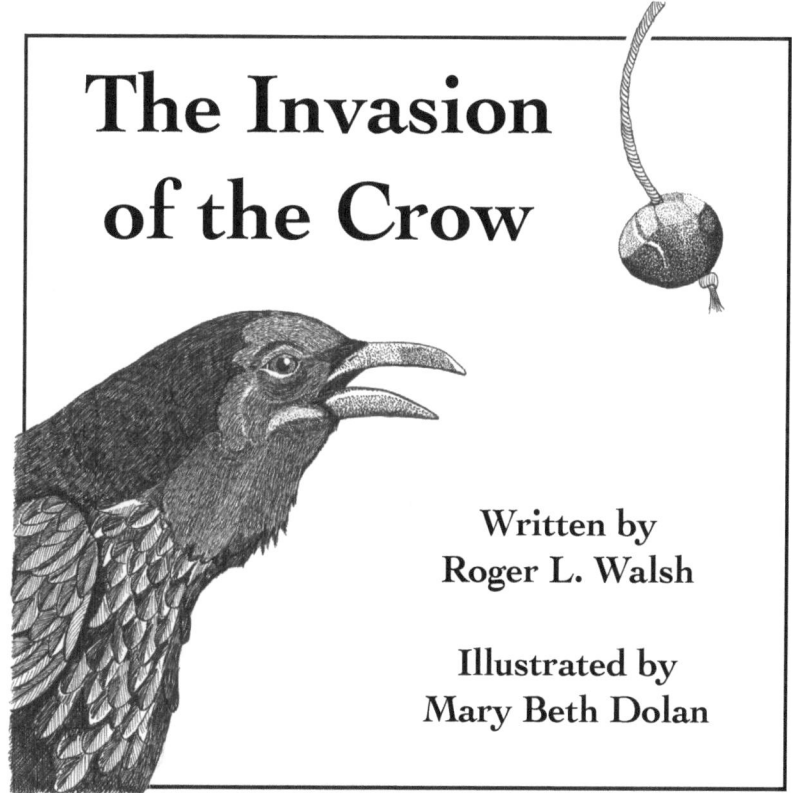

Written by
Roger L. Walsh

Illustrated by
Mary Beth Dolan

To order additional copies of this book, contact:
Xlibris Corporation
1-888-795-4274
www.Xlibris.com
Orders@Xlibris.com

Dedicated to:
Devin, Owen and Evelyn

I will always remember that hot, sultry summer's day when the crow's call outside my bedroom window awoke me. The grass had started to turn brown, which was a bit unusual for that time of year, but the sun had been shining a great deal and the rainfall had been sparse. The heavy air seemed to enfold a person's being, almost to the point of being crushing. Any slight movement would bring out sweat that would cause my clothes to stick to me, making me feel dirty all of the time.

I was living in anticipation of the Fourth of July celebration which brought with it the excitement of fireworks, parades and the annual carnival that would come to town, with its rides, cotton candy and red juicy apples on a stick dipped in caramel. It was a break in the summer vacation time when lots of us boys would be getting bored with having nothing to do. If we hung around our houses too much our parents would find more chores than ever for us to do to "keep us occupied" and out of trouble.

The crow was a bit of a show-off, dressed in his finest ebony-hued garb, as he fluttered and strutted into every back yard in the neighborhood. Some folks said that crows are evil birds

and bring misfortune with them, and it didn't take long before people were talking about shooting him, since their repeated "shoo, -shoo, -shoo's" didn't keep him away for long. He would keep coming back, swooping down at someone's cat, and ladies would screech and holler, "Watch out, he'll poke your eyes out. He's a mean one."

I sort of admired this magnificent bird as he would put on his act of derring-do, to the delight of most of the boys my age. (I was twelve, approaching thirteen and was beginning to test my own wings at that time by being rebellious and belligerent, especially when it came to "others' imposed" rules.) The crow flew wherever he wanted to go. He landed on trees, on housetops, and quite often on the ground. Then he would, with much bravado, stalk a cat or dog and give them a playful peck, and they would respond noisily with a sudden squawk or yelp. The little kids were afraid of the crow and frightened mothers would keep youngsters indoors, which interrupted their daily routines.

The adventurous crow kept us all captivated in one way or another for several days. It was fun for me to witness all of the futile attempts of others as they tried so many ways to get rid of the pesky bird. I began to think that the crow had a very distinct personality, that he was having as much enjoyment as he possibly could, at the expense of the neighbors, their pets and children. I noticed that the glossy coat of feathers on the crow seemed to be shinier and in better condition than any other crow I had ever seen. I spent hours just watching as his every movement and sound captured my imagination.

He had been around since Monday. On Friday, the day before the Fourth of July, I was sitting on the back porch swing, watching the crow. I noticed that he liked to inspect shining objects at great length. His head would turn to one side, then cock the other way as he swaggered and strutted closer, closer, closer to anything that shined. I decided to test him to see if I could get him interested in some of the horse-chestnuts that I had saved since the year before. The chestnuts were well-polished. I liked to think of them as being precious stones of great value and would often take a soft cloth and rub them until they glowed. I placed a few chestnuts on the ground, and I drove a nail through some so I could put a piece of string through their centers for hanging. The chestnuts, both on the ground and the swinging ones, caught the crow's attention. Strut, strut, swagger, swagger.

The crow came closer and closer to inspect the chestnuts. He pecked at one on a string. It swung away from him and then straight back towards him. He was so quick as he leaped into the air and with a flutter of wings was gone, up to safety on the roof of our house. Within a few minutes he was back again, approaching slowly and seemingly more alert and watchful than before. I watched intently, not moving so I wouldn't scare him away. I watched and watched as he mustered up his courage and pecked again at one of the swinging chestnuts. It swung away and then back, but this time, instead of flying away, he just quickly jumped to one side as the chestnut swung harmlessly past his head. Then something very strange happened. He looked right at me, fixing his eyes on mine as though to say, "You haven't fooled me. I knew you were there all the time," and then he said, "Hello. Hello. Hello."

I couldn't believe my ears and there was no one else to hear. I told myself that I must be imagining things. After a few more pecks at the chestnuts, the crow, seeing the

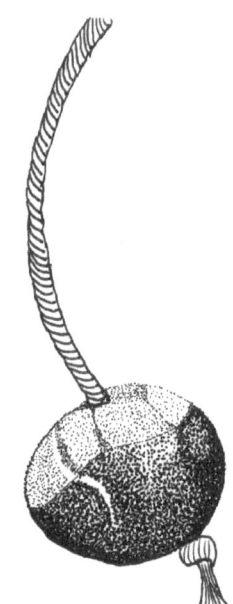

impossibility of the situation, decided to fly away. He was gone for the rest of the day.

That evening at supper, I told my Dad about the crow and the chestnuts. Dad knew a lot about birds. Even so, I was still very much amazed at his response when I told him the crow had said "hello" to me. He said, "I'm not surprised. Did you notice that he seems to be unafraid of people and pets? I think someone had him as a pet and either he escaped or they let him go." Then Dad told me that some people would capture a baby crow and keep it as a pet. "Quite often," he said, "you can teach a crow to mimic some words. Unfortunately, in order to create a 'voice box' for the crow, their captors split the crow's tongue down the middle." Dad liked birds so I knew even without asking that that was a cruel thing to do and he didn't approve of it.

After supper, the family gathered on the front porch as we did on those hot summer nights. The front of the house faced due west, and evening after evening we would just sit quietly and watch the sun set. Mom sometimes would serve us some sort of dessert: pie, cake or ice cream. I would dream of far away places and of things I wanted to do. People would often walk by and say, "How do you do?" Sometimes they would join us on the porch to be served some of what it was that we were having. So, it wasn't unusual that Friday evening, the evening before the Fourth of July, to see more activity than usual as the neighborhood seemed to be buzzing with excitement about plans for the next day: the fireworks, parades and carnival. But, actually, the talking was not about any celebration. People were talking about how to get rid of that pesky crow. Some people spoke softly and others (my, how they carried on) talked about shooting him.

Dad and I walked over to where the commotion was. After we listened to the excited and sometimes heated debate about the crow, Dad asked if anyone had a cage large enough for the crow. His plan was to capture the crow and drive him far into the country and let him go. A neighbor spoke up and said, "I have a large cage, but I would rather shoot him and be done with it, tomorrow if at all possible. Besides, who would catch the crow and cage him?" Dad told the man to at least give us a chance. All of the men in the neighborhood would be home tomorrow since they had the day off, and surely they could

work it out together. Some of the men still wanted to shoot the crow, plain and simple. It would be over so quickly and they could get on with their big plans for the Fourth. After all, it wasn't fair for them to have to waste a day off on some stupid crow.

Large cage in hand, Dad and I walked home. We hoped we would be given a chance to catch the crow, save him from execution and set him free somewhere miles from home. Our problem then was: how would we catch the crow? I went to bed and spent quite a restless night. I tossed and turned in bed, trying to imagine how it could possibly be done. Finally, just before dawn, I could see what had to be done in order to catch the crow. Then, for a few hours, I slept soundly, as though I knew my plan would work.

The next morning, my mother called me for breakfast and I was up like a shot. Dressed in an old t-shirt and jeans, I raced downstairs to share my "crow-capture" plan with Dad. I reminded him about the day before, when the crow's curiosity forced him to investigate the shiny horse-chestnuts. Dad said, "Crows are a wary sort of bird, not easily fooled. If you think he will just go into the cage by himself, well, it might work, but I don't think so. We have to think of a way to first catch the crow, then put him into the cage."

"I've got it!" I shrieked. "I will cut the largest chestnut in two, hold one half in one hand and when he comes to take a peck of the tasty insides, I'll grab him with my free hand! Then we can put him into the cage." Dad said, "I don't really like it, but you can try. If it doesn't work, we'll have to think of something else."

By closely watching the crow's habits during the week, I knew he would start his usual rounds in the vicinity of the dirt road that ran behind our house and the neighbors' houses. It was nearly eight o'clock in the morning and I could already hear firecrackers going off in the distance. I carried my chestnuts up to the road wrapped in my old large red handkerchief. I had already picked out the largest one, cut it in two, and polished all of the others that would be used as additional bait to lure the crow to my hand.

Once upon the dirt road, I picked out a spot where I would lie and spread the chestnuts around my hands, holding the half chestnut in my left hand. That spot would be in the sun for most of the day, bright enough to reflect sparkling, inviting rays to attract the attention of the crow.

So, finally I settled down in the dust of the road, flat on my stomach with my face resting on the red handkerchief. Arms outstretched, my vigil began. I waited and waited and waited. A slight breeze would gently blow dust in my ears from time to time. I was determined. "Okay, Mr. Crow. It's me and you. A duel in the sun." Waiting, waiting, waiting.

By nine o'clock my arms and legs were getting numb, but I knew he was there watching, watching, watching. I knew sooner or later his curiosity would get the best of him and he would simply have to investigate. Finally, he flew overhead, then made a second pass, then a third, landing on the ground at a safe distance from me. People were gathering, hiding behind trees, barns and garages, reporting back and forth to one another: "See the crow?" "See the boy in the roadside?" "I wouldn't do it." "Let's just shoot the crow." "Isn't it hot?"

"How can he stand it so long?"

The battle of the wills had now begun. The crow moved closer, closer, closer. Looking at the chestnuts, then at me. Back and forth, back and forth. Strut, strut. Swagger, swagger. Later, I could sense that the sun had risen directly above me. My bare face and arms began to hurt, scorched by the heat from the sun. I could sense the dust up my nostrils, and my legs began to tremble as though they had a mind of their own. Strut, strut, jump back. I could hear the distant murmuring of the people. Strut, strut, swagger, swagger. Then I felt it. After all this time, a peck, square in the center of the chestnut in my hand. Now the rhythm changed. Strut, strut, peck, jump back. I watched now, closer than before. The crow was pecking, not just once, but peck, peck, jump back, peck, peck, jump. I knew it was time.

The crow was fully concentrating on the chestnut and I on him. Here he comes. Strut, strut, peck, peck, pec... I grabbed him with my free hand around his spindly legs. He began to flap his wings, raising up a lot of dust and pecking me violently. Peck, peck, peck, peck. Little holes were rapidly appearing in the back of my hand, the blood flowing.

I heard a voice. It was Dad. "Don't let go! Don't let go!" He was there in an instant, quickly wrapping a large towel around the crow and lifting it from my hand. He shoved the crow, towel and all, into the cage and slammed the door shut. The crow was captured.

People began to emerge from their hiding places where they had been watching the proceedings. Some were cheering, especially the little children because now they had their freedom to play outdoors again.

After I had a bath and lunch, we put the cage into the back of a neighbor's pick-up truck and drove out into the country about ten miles. Before setting the crow free, my dad checked its tongue and sure enough, it had been split so it could talk.

The memory of that Fourth of July has been special to me. We celebrated the freedom of our country, and the freedom of the kids and pets in the neighborhood. But, I remember celebrating that day with a wild creature who took back the sky and announced his freedom from a branch high in a tree, almost mockingly to us, saying loudly, "Hello. Hello. Hello."

I was regarded as a neighborhood hero for just a few days. Then everything was back to normal. The sun was hot, the summer was long, and we had nothing to do.

Roger L. Walsh was born 1939 in Leigh, Lancashire, England. He moved to the United States with his family in 1947.

Roger learned to enjoy storytelling from his Mother while in England during WWII. "Mom was our nightly entertainment in the living room by the fire. She recited or read poetry that she had loved since her childhood."

Education has always been a big part of Roger's life. "At age four, I learned to make the alphabet with modeling clay, since we had no paper or pencils."

Roger graduated from Vandergrift High School in 1956 and from Pittsburgh Technical Institute in 1957. He entered Roberts Wesleyan College, Rochester, New York, in 1960. He graduated in 1965, with a BS in Psychology, minor in Biology.

In 1969, Roger graduated from State University of New York at Oneonta with an MS in Education. He attended the PhD program in Education at Syracuse University from 1972-75.

As an educator, Roger began teaching in Pittsburgh, Pennsylvania in 1965. He later moved to Herkimer, New York, then to Fort Myers, Florida. He returned to New York to become a school principal at East Palmyra Christian school.

Today he teaches at Empire State College, State University of New York.

Roger has taught "Writing Your Memoirs" for the past twenty-five years. "The Invasion of the Crow" was written as an example of story telling for his students. He has other stories and poetry as well.

Mary Beth Dolan has always been fascinated by animals and nature. As a teenager she would spend entire afternoons drawing what she saw in the woods around her home. After obtaining a degree in Advertising Design and Production, she has continued to create artwork professionally. This is her first book illustration job.

Still a nature lover, she lives in western New York; and continues to bring her sketchbook on hiking trips.

Visit Mary Beth online at:
www.startherestudio.com